W9-BJH-651

Harriet Beecher Stowe

Author of Uncle Tom's Cabin

Colonial Leaders

Lord Baltimore
English Politician and Colonist

Benjamin Banneker
American Mathematician and Astronomer

Sir William Berkeley
Governor of Virginia

William Bradford
Governor of Plymouth Colony

Jonathan Edwards
Colonial Religious Leader

Benjamin Franklin
American Statesman, Scientist, and Writer

Anne Hutchinson
Religious Leader

Cotton Mather
Author, Clergyman, and Scholar

Increase Mather
Clergyman and Scholar

James Oglethorpe
Humanitarian and Soldier

William Penn
Founder of Democracy

Sir Walter Raleigh
English Explorer and Author

Caesar Rodney
American Patriot

John Smith
English Explorer and Colonist

Miles Standish
Plymouth Colony Leader

Peter Stuyvesant
Dutch Military Leader

George Whitefield
Clergyman and Scholar

Roger Williams
Founder of Rhode Island

John Winthrop
Politician and Statesman

John Peter Zenger
Free Press Advocate

Revolutionary War Leaders

John Adams
Second U.S. President

Ethan Allen
Revolutionary Hero

Benedict Arnold
Traitor to the Cause

King George III
English Monarch

Nathanael Greene
Military Leader

Nathan Hale
Revolutionary Hero

Alexander Hamilton
First U.S. Secretary of the Treasury

John Hancock
President of the Continental Congress

Patrick Henry
American Statesman and Speaker

John Jay
First Chief Justice of the Supreme Court

Thomas Jefferson
Author of the Declaration of Independence

John Paul Jones
Father of the U.S. Navy

Lafayette
French Freedom Fighter

James Madison
Father of the Constitution

Francis Marion
The Swamp Fox

James Monroe
American Statesman

Thomas Paine
Political Writer

Paul Revere
American Patriot

Betsy Ross
American Patriot

George Washington
First U.S. President

Famous Figures of the Civil War Era

Jefferson Davis
Confederate President

Frederick Douglass
Abolitionist and Author

Ulysses S. Grant
Military Leader and President

Stonewall Jackson
Confederate General

Robert E. Lee
Confederate General

Abraham Lincoln
Civil War President

William Sherman
Union General

Harriet Beecher Stowe
Author of Uncle Tom's Cabin

Sojourner Truth
Abolitionist, Suffragist, and Preacher

Harriet Tubman
Leader of the Underground Railroad

Famous Figures of the Civil War Era

Harriet Beecher Stowe

Author of Uncle Tom's Cabin

LeeAnne Gelletly

Arthur M. Schlesinger, jr.
Senior Consulting Editor

Chelsea House Publishers

Philadelphia

Produced by 21st Century Publishing and Communications, Inc.
New York, NY. http://www.21cpc.com

CHELSEA HOUSE PUBLISHERS
Production Manager Pamela Loos
Art Director Sara Davis
Director of Photography Judy L. Hasday
Managing Editor James D. Gallagher
Senior Production Editor J. Christopher Higgins

Staff for *HARRIET BEECHER STOWE*
Project Editor Anne Hill
Associate Art Director Takeshi Takahashi
Series Design Keith Trego

The Chelsea House World Wide Web address is
http://www.chelseahouse.com

First Printing
3 5 7 9 8 6 4 2

Library of Congress Cataloging-in-Publication Data

Gelletly, LeeAnne.
    Harriet Beecher Stowe / LeeAnne Gelletly.
        p.   cm. — (Famous figures of the Civil War era)
    Includes bibliographical references (p.   ) and index.
    ISBN 0-7910-6009-8
        1. Stowe, Harriet Beecher, 1811-1896—Juvenile literature. 2. United
States—History—Civil War, 1861-1865—Literature and the war—Juvenile
literature. 3. Authors, American—19th century—Biography—Juvenile
literature. 4. Abolitionists—United States—Biography—Juvenile literature.
[1. Stowe, Harriet Beecher, 1811-1896. 2. Authors, American. 3. Women—
Biography.] I. Title. II. Series.

PS2956 .G36   2000
813'.3—dc21   00-038380
[B]   CIP

Contents

Harriet Beecher Stowe was born in a small New England town much like this one. No one could have guessed that the Beechers' baby girl would grow up to be one of America's most influential writers.

A New England Beginning

On the bright early summer day of June 14, 1811, the cries of a newborn baby girl echoed through the **parsonage** in Litchfield, Connecticut. The infant's father, Lyman Beecher, was a well-known **Congregationalist** minister. He and his wife Roxana Foote named their daughter Harriet Elizabeth Beecher.

Lyman Beecher, born in 1775, was the son and grandson of blacksmiths. Instead of following in his father's and grandfather's footsteps, he had become a minister. As a preacher for the Congregationalist Church, he wanted to save souls and reform the nation. Almost everyone in New England knew about Pastor Beecher's powerful sermons.

Roxana was a granddaughter of General Andrew Ward, who had served under George Washington during America's Revolutionary War. Roxana was an intelligent woman. She read many books and also had learned to speak French.

As a minister's wife, Roxana was very busy. She didn't have much time for anything but doing household chores and caring for children. However, she also ran a boardinghouse. The family's two-story house overflowed with young children, visitors, teachers, and students from nearby schools.

But Harriet would never get to know her mother very well. The little girl was not quite five years old when Roxana developed **tuberculosis,** a disease of the lungs. No one knew what caused the illness or how to treat it at the time. She died in September 1816. Her last wish was that all her sons would become preachers.

Roxana left her husband with many children. The two older girls were Catharine and Mary. The three older boys were William, Edward, and George.

Two more brothers–Henry Ward and Charles– joined the family after Harriet was born. As a young child, Harriet was closest to Henry.

Lyman Beecher remarried a year after his wife died. His new wife, Harriet Porter, was kind to her stepchildren, but she was never close to them. Soon she began having children of her own. Her first son, Frederick, was followed by Isabella, Thomas, and James. Harriet grew up with a total of seven brothers and three sisters.

At the age of eight, Harriet began school at the nearby Litchfield Female Academy. Her father also taught his children at home. He liked to make them think. Whenever the family got together, whether at the dinner table or while doing chores, he asked questions and debated with the boys.

The fiery preacher shared his first wife's vision. He wanted his sons to become ministers, as he was. But he did not have great plans for his daughters. American women didn't have many roles to choose from in the early 1800s except those of wife and mother. It was not acceptable for a woman to stand up in public and speak. Women could not even lead a prayer in church, much less become ministers.

That's probably why Pastor Beecher liked his boys more than his girls. Harriet knew she would always have to work extra hard to please her father. That became her goal. She would take on tasks that her brothers normally did. She thought that if she chopped and stacked the firewood, just maybe her father would notice her.

Sometimes it worked. Harriet remembered one day of cutting and piling the wood. Afterward her father commented that she had done the best job of all the children. He gave her his highest compliment when he said, "You would have made the best boy of the lot."

Lyman Beecher was a nationally known preacher. Many of his children would also grow up to become famous. His son Henry was called the greatest preacher of his day. Edward, also a minister, became a college president. Catharine supported a woman's right to an education. Isabella believed in women's **suffrage**, or the right to vote. She worked in the early days of the suffrage movement. And Harriet became a world-famous author.

Harriet loved to read, and once read her favorite book, *Ivanhoe*, seven times in one month.

Sometimes Harriet escaped from the large, noisy household by spending time in her father's study. In later years, she would describe how she enjoyed spending time in that room surrounded by the "friendly, quiet faces of books."

In the peaceful study, Harriet could lose herself in the world of *The Arabian Nights.* She might dwell on the romantic poetry of Lord Byron or travel with the medieval knights of Sir Walter Scott's *Ivanhoe.* Harriet enjoyed *Ivanhoe* so much that at the age of 12, she read it seven times in one month.

Harriet attended the Litchfield Female Academy for several years. Her best subject was writing, which she did far better than most girls her age. One time Pastor Beecher was present when a student's essay was read aloud. The minister was impressed by the work and asked who had written it. Harriet beamed as her teacher replied, "Your daughter, sir." In later years, she would retell that story, recounting it as "the proudest moment" in her life.

When Harriet was 13, she went to a new school, the Hartford Female Seminary. The year before, her 23-year-old sister Catharine had opened the seminary, which was run for and by women. The seminary served students ages 12 and up.

Catharine wanted her school to build its pupils' characters, improve their knowledge, and prepare them to enter society. Harriet's sister Mary also helped teach there. In its first year, the school had only seven students. But the following year, when Harriet arrived, 25 new pupils were enrolled.

At first, Harriet was only a student. But the following year, she began teaching other students. Some of those girls were her own age. Between teaching and studying, Harriet had little time for herself. She got up before sunrise and spent the whole day either attending or teaching classes. In the evening she studied Latin and mathematics and prepared the next day's lessons.

Harriet also took drawing lessons, beginning a hobby that she would continue for the rest of her life. She studied art because she thought she would teach it at her sister's school. But she ended up teaching what she herself did best: writing and composition. In a few short years, Harriet finished her studies at Hartford Female Seminary and was

When Harriet's family moved to Cincinnati, Ohio, they rode in a coach over rough roads. The journey was long and tiresome.

teaching full time. But she did not stay long.

In early 1832, Lyman Beecher received an offer to become president of Lane Seminary. The school was located in Cincinnati, Ohio. In the early 1800s, Cincinnati was considered to be part of the West.

Pastor Beecher was thrilled to have the opportunity to run a college that trained ministers. He could shape the religious future of the country. His daughters Catharine and Harriet decided to join him on this new adventure. Catharine was eager to open up a new school in the West. Harriet, at age 21, was ready for a change as well.

Ten members of the Beecher family traveled to Cincinnati together. The rest stayed behind. The family traveled first by steamboat from Boston to Philadelphia. In Philadelphia, Pastor Beecher stopped for a while to preach and raise funds for his new school.

Next came an eight-day stagecoach ride. It was not a smooth journey, especially in Virginia and Ohio. Roads in those states were covered with rough logs to keep the wagon wheels from getting stuck in mud. Because of the lines of logs those routes were called "corduroy roads." After several days of bouncing and jolting over the bumpy roads, the exhausted Beecher family was relieved to finally reach its new home.

This picture of Cincinnati, Ohio, dates from the 1830s. There, Harriet saw slaves for the first time and realized she would always oppose the practice of slavery.

A Writer
and a Mother

When Lyman Beecher brought his family to Cincinnati, Ohio, it was one of the fastest-growing cities in the nation. Located on the northern bank of the Ohio River, Cincinnati was a center for shipping. It featured stately buildings and elegant homes. Some people called it the "Queen City of the West."

But Cincinnati also contained **slaughterhouses** and pork-processing plants. Hogs roamed the city, rooting in the many piles of stinking garbage dumped out onto the streets from the nearby homes. This gave Cincinnati another nickname as well: "Porkopolis."

During the spring of 1832, a few months before the

Beechers arrived, Cincinnati experienced one of its worst floods in history. Many businesses near the Ohio River were covered with water. It took weeks for the water to settle back within the river banks and for residents to clean up all the buildings.

Just as the city was recovering, **cholera** struck. Cholera is a deadly disease. Early symptoms include diarrhea, vomiting, stomach cramps, and cold hands and feet. People did not understand that the piles of rotting garbage spread the disease. No one knew about germs that could travel through the air or dirty drinking water. More than 800 people in Cincinnati died of cholera during the 1832 epidemic.

In November of that year the Beechers arrived in the city. Both their new home and the Lane Seminary were located in Walnut Hills. This wooded community overlooked the city and was protected from flooding. Catharine set up her new school, Western Female Institute, nearby. Harriet soon began teaching six days a week there.

Harriet also wanted to be a writer. Shortly

As a young woman, Harriet taught in a small, one-room schoolhouse much like this one. Teachers often worked six days a week.

after arriving in Cincinnati, she published a text-book, *Primary Geography for Children*. It sold very well and she received $187 for the work. That was almost as much as her older sister made in one year of running her school.

Harriet wanted more practice writing, so she joined a literary group called the Semi-Colon

Club. Its members included James Hall, the editor of a new magazine, *Western Monthly.* Calvin Ellis Stowe, a teacher at Lane Seminary, and his wife, Eliza Tyler, were also members. Calvin was a clergyman. He taught biblical literature at the seminary. Eliza shared many of Harriet's interests, and the two women quickly became good friends.

At meetings, the members would read aloud and discuss stories they had written. James Hall liked one of Harriet's short stories so much that he encouraged her to enter it in a competition run by his magazine. Harriet's story won first prize. It was published in the April 1834 issue of the magazine. The excited author knew she would publish many more articles in the years to come.

Most of Harriet's first stories were short compositions called **sketches**. In them, she described people she and her family had known in New England. Soon, she began also writing about what she saw while living in the West.

In Cincinnati, for the first time, Harriet was exposed to slavery, the act of owning another human being. Most Northern states had outlawed slavery. They were called **free states**. But the South contained **slave states**, where slavery was legal. Slaves provided cheap labor for work on huge cotton and tobacco **plantations**. Most wealthy white Southerners thought slavery was necessary to their way of life. They believed that without slaves, they wouldn't be able to run their plantations.

Only a few reformers tried to abolish, or end, slavery. They were called **abolitionists.** They held meetings, gave speeches, and organized rallies against the evils of slavery. Some distributed anti-slavery books, newspapers, and pamphlets.

Most people thought abolitionists were just troublemakers. Many Northerners thought the problem of slavery would probably go away by itself. Others didn't think much about it at all.

Although Cincinnati was in the free state of Ohio, the slave state of Kentucky was just across the Ohio River. This location made Cincinnati a center of the conflict over slavery. The city was an important part of the **Underground Railroad.**

The Underground Railroad was not really a railroad. It was a route used by slaves escaping to the North. On the route were a series of stations, where slaves could find food and clothing.

A famous leader of the Underground Railroad was another woman named Harriet. Harriet Tubman was black and had been a slave herself. Like Harriet Beecher Stowe, Harriet Tubman was small—just five feet tall. But she was strong and a fighter. After escaping to the North, she risked recapture and even death by returning to the South 19 more times and helping lead more than 300 slaves to freedom.

Many of Cincinnati's shipping businesses relied on work from Southern states. So the owners didn't want to create problems with their customers in the South. Some leaders even tried to stop abolitionists.

In the city Harriet saw notices that posted large rewards for runaway slaves. From the banks of the Ohio River, Harriet saw boatloads of chained slaves being carried downriver to be sold in the South. She also heard of slave hunters, who would catch runaway slaves for rewards. She learned that even free blacks were sometimes captured.

In June 1833, Harriet visited the home of one of her students in Kentucky. The journey gave Harriet a firsthand look at slavery in the South. At her host's elegant plantation, Harriet saw slaves treated kindly. But when she visited a neighboring plantation, she saw the owner abuse his slaves. Harriet never forgot how upset she felt.

That same summer Harriet and her father visited the home of a family friend, Mr. Rankin. He was a Presbyterian minister whose house stood at the top of a steep hill overlooking the Ohio River. As the minister placed a lamp in his window, he explained to his guests that the light was a signal. It told runaway slaves who were crossing the river that his home was a station of the Underground Railroad. They would find food and shelter there.

Rankin told the true story of a slave trying to escape. One night in early spring, a young woman carrying her baby appeared at his doorstep. She had just managed to find her way across the semi frozen river. He took the

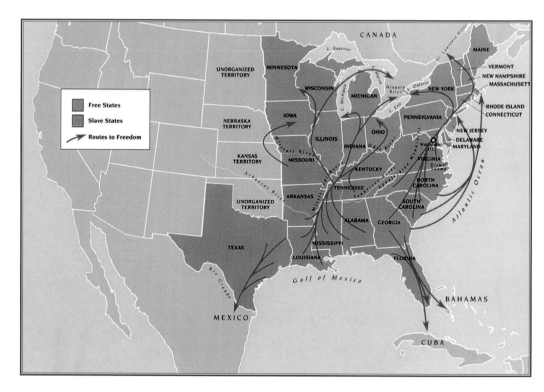

This map of the Underground Railroad shows the routes slaves took to freedom. Harriet later used stories of slave escapes in her writing.

woman to the next stop and returned home.

Then he heard a loud noise coming up from the river. It was the sound of cracking ice and rushing water. The frozen river was breaking up. The runaway slave had crossed the ice to safety just in time. Anyone still out on the river would certainly have drowned.

In 1834, Harriet traveled back East to visit relatives and friends. A few months later she returned to Cincinnati with her brother Henry. He was planning to enter Lane Seminary.

But that summer, Lane Seminary had run into trouble. The board of trustees had voted to prevent abolitionist students from holding anti-slavery meetings. This angered many of the students. Most of them protested by leaving the school. The seminary's main financial supporter was also an abolitionist. When he learned what the trustees had done, he withdrew his funding. The school was near **bankruptcy**.

There was more bad news. While Harriet was gone, her good friend Eliza Stowe had died from cholera. Harriet and Eliza's husband, Calvin Stowe, helped each other cope with the loss of Eliza. The two friends spent a great deal of time together. Over the next year and a half, their friendship grew. Eventually it blossomed into love.

On January 6, 1836, Harriet and Calvin were married. Harriet stopped teaching and began using her time for writing. A few months later, Calvin left for a trip to England to purchase books for the seminary.

While Calvin was away, tempers in Cincinnati began to flare over the issue of slavery. That summer James G. Birney, a lawyer, had begun publishing an important abolitionist paper called the *Philanthropist*. On a hot July night, a pro-slavery mob broke into the newspaper office and attacked the presses.

Harriet's brother Henry was upset. He wrote an editorial in another newspaper, defending freedom of speech. In response, the unruly crowd gathered again and destroyed the *Philanthropist* office. They smashed the printing press and threw it into the river.

The riot spilled over into the rest of the city. Mobs attacked black families' homes in a section of the city called "Little Africa." They set some of the homes on fire. Other newspaper offices were also threatened. The rioting lasted for three nights.

Harriet was horrified by the violence. Slavery

bothered her, but she was confused about what she could do. "No one can have the system of slavery brought before him without an irrepressible desire to *do* something," she wrote, "but what is there to be done?" At the moment, she had no answer.

Harriet's own family life soon took up most of her time and attention. In September 1836, she had twin girls. Calvin was still away when the babies were born. Harriet named one daughter Eliza Tyler, after Calvin's first wife, and named the other Isabella Beecher. Upon his return, Calvin declared that if one child was named for his first wife, the second should be named for his second wife. So Isabella was renamed Harriet.

That same year, Harriet's brother Edward began working for the abolitionist movement in Alton, Illinois, helping Elijah Lovejoy publish an antislavery newspaper. Soon afterward, news reached the Beecher family in Cincinnati that a furious proslavery mob had stormed the newspaper office where Edward worked. Both Elijah and Edward had been killed. Harriet was stunned. A few days later, the family was relieved to learn that Edward was alive after all. But his friend Elijah had indeed lost his life.

The Stowes were having money problems. Calvin didn't make much money as a teacher and was not good at managing what he had. With all the controversy over slavery, the school had few students and did not have enough money to pay him.

To help make ends meet, Harriet turned to selling stories and articles. With the extra money, she could afford to hire a house servant. The extra help proved useful. Just 15 months after the twins' birth, their third child, Henry Ellis, was born.

Harriet's life became a whirlwind. For the next 11 years, she plunged into an exhausting cycle of writing, caring for children, and having babies. Frederick William was born in 1840, followed by Georgiana May in 1843 and Samuel Charles in 1848.

Family life was important to Harriet. She was very proud of her role as a wife and mother.

Along with everything else that was happening in her life, Harriet had the exciting experience of seeing her first fiction book published. In 1842, Catharine, who had been writing and publishing "how to" books for women, showed some of Harriet's short stories to a publisher. The following year, Harper & Brothers published Harriet's stories in a book called *The Mayflower: Sketches of Scenes and Characters Among the Descendants of the Pilgrims.*

During this time, slavery became much more personal than Harriet had ever dreamed it would. Her servant girl had claimed to be free but later admitted that she was actually an escaped slave. She told Harriet that her owner was in town looking for her. If she were caught, she would be returned to slavery and might even be killed. Terrified, the girl pleaded with Harriet for help.

That night, Calvin and Henry Beecher hid the escaped slave in a wagon and drove her to the safety of an Underground Railroad station.

In the summer of 1849, yet another cholera epidemic swept through Cincinnati. This time the illness struck two of Harriet's children: 18-month-old Charley and 11-year-old Henry. The older boy recovered, but Charley died two weeks later. The loss of her son burned in Harriet's heart for years to come.

Calvin had been away on business when

Charley died. Harriet wrote to him about the news and encouraged him to finish his business. Her neighbors and family were providing comfort. When Calvin did return from his trip, he brought news of his own. He had been offered a teaching post at Bowdoin College in Brunswick, Maine. Having lived in Cincinnati for 18 years, Harriet was eager to return to New England.

The Stowe family moved to Maine in the summer of 1850. There Harriet gave birth to her seventh child, Charles Edward. She helped Catharine begin yet another school. And of course, she kept writing. Harriet would also find the answer to the question of what she could do to help end slavery.

In the South, slaves worked in the cotton fields. Plantation owners depended on slaves' hard work to grow their crops, so they did not want to see slavery abolished.

3

Accursed Slavery

Slavery had existed in America since the arrival of the first English and Spanish settlers. Over the years, more than nine million Africans had been kidnapped from their homes and crammed into ships headed for America. Once they reached the United States, they were bought at auctions and became slaves.

In the South, one out of four white families owned black slaves. These slaves cared for their masters' households or worked in the fields. Most of the slaves worked on cotton plantations. They lived in small, crude cabins and owned one or two sets of clothing.

Six days a week, they worked from dawn to dusk. Often they were under the threat of being whipped or another form of severe punishment.

Some people had tried to outlaw slavery before the Revolutionary War. The first formal protest against slavery was made in 1688 by a group of Quakers in Pennsylvania. Quakers are a Christian group whose members also oppose war. In 1726, colonists in Virginia asked the British government to stop the kidnapping and enslavement of Africans. But slavery still continued.

By the 1820s, 147 groups were working to end slavery in America. The antislavery movement was growing quickly. By the 1830s, reformers had created 1,350 antislavery societies. These societies were made up of a wide variety of people, including free blacks, escaped slaves, Native Americans, and white people who simply believed slavery was wrong. Some of their supporters risked their lives to help slaves escape through the Underground Railroad.

The groups proposed many different ways to end slavery, but the abolitionists were the most **radical**. They believed slaves should be freed right away and allowed to live wherever they wished.

Everyone in the Beecher family opposed slavery, although in different ways. Harriet's father and stepmother took the more conservative view. They supported the idea that slaves be freed gradually. Then they would be returned to Africa to establish new places to live. But Harriet's two older brothers, George and Edward Beecher, were strong abolitionists who believed that slavery had to end immediately. Harriet also believed that all slaves should be **emancipated**, or set free, immediately.

In the middle of the 1800s, many new states were joining the Union. The issue of slavery was on everyone's minds. Leaders of Congress argued over the status of the new states of Missouri, Texas, Kansas, and Nebraska. Some **legislators** wanted all western states to be free. But the South demanded that some be slave states, too.

In 1849, the people of California voted to enter

the Union as a free state. Many Southern states did not like this idea. Some even threatened to **secede,** or break away, from the Union. To keep the Union together, Congress made a deal. California could enter as a free state, and at the same time, legislators would create a strict slavery law.

In 1850, Congress passed the **Fugitive Slave Act**. It was signed into law by President Millard Fillmore. The law required that any **fugitive** or runaway slave found in the North must be sent back South. Southern slave owners could catch fugitive slaves in free states. Anyone caught helping runaway slaves would be punished by a heavy fine and jail sentence.

People in the North were

An editor in Massachusetts, William Lloyd Garrison was put in jail for **libeling a merchant** who was helping fugitive slaves. Upon his release from prison, Garrison published the first issue of his antislavery newspaper, the *Liberator,* on New Year's Day 1831. He would publish the *Liberator* for the next 30 years.

In 1833, Garrison founded the American Anti-Slavery Society. Its membership rose to nearly 250,000 in five years. It was the first American organization in which blacks as well as whites, and woman as well as men, played an active role.

horrified. The act seemed to make slavery legal in the North. The Fugitive Slave Act made many Northerners angry enough to join the abolitionist movement.

Harriet's brother Edward was now an outspoken abolitionist living in Boston. He knew many fugitive slaves and had a library of their writings. On a visit to Edward's home, Harriet learned about the **autobiography** written by one former slave.

Josiah Henson had been a slave in Kentucky. Once beaten so badly that his shoulders were broken, he was determined to escape slavery. Henson first tried to purchase his freedom by working for other people to earn the necessary $600. But his owner then doubled the price and even threatened to sell him. Instead Henson escaped with his family to Canada. There he became a minister and abolitionist.

Harriet was impressed with Henson's story. She also could not forget the loss she felt when her son Charley died. She explained these feelings

Slave owners often took children from their mothers. This horrified Harriet, who remembered the pain of losing her own son.

about Charley in a letter written to her friend Eliza Cabot Follen: "It was at his dying bed and at his grave that I learned what a poor slave mother may feel when her child is torn away from her."

In 1857, Harriet received a letter from Edward's wife, Isabella. She wrote to Harriet about scenes in Boston, where because of the Fugitive Slave Act, blacks were being captured and taken back into slavery. Some of them had never lived in the South or been slaves. It was terrible that federal troops could enforce such a law.

Isabella finished her letter with these words, "Hattie, if I could use a pen as you can, I would write something that would make this whole nation feel what an **accursed** thing slavery is."

Harriet knew Isabella was right. She had to help end slavery. But what could she write?

Runaway slaves like these faced danger every day in their flight toward freedom. Harriet dramatized their stories in her book *Uncle Tom's Cabin*.

Uncle Tom's Cabin

Like her father, Harriet understood that words have power. She used pen and ink, while her father used his gift of speaking. Inspired by Isabella's letter, Harriet started thinking about what she could write. She wanted to say something that would reach people, something that would open their eyes.

For several months, she could not figure out what to say. Then, one February day, a picture formed in her mind while she was sitting quietly at church. As her youngest son, Charles, would later describe the event, a vivid scene had "blown into her mind as by the rushing of a mighty wind." Harriet hurried home and scribbled down her vision in a story.

In her mind, she had seen an old black slave being whipped to death by two other slaves. A white man, the slave's owner, was cruelly urging them on. But the dying slave's last words weren't about hatred. Instead they expressed his religious faith. With shaking hands, Harriet finished her powerful story. She read it aloud to her children. But then she set it aside, not sure what to do with it.

Months passed. Then one day her husband came across the manuscript. After reading it, he urged Harriet to use the short story as the powerful, final scene of a much longer tale. This was the idea Harriet had needed.

She began writing in earnest, creating separate episodes for a weekly newspaper. Harriet sent the first part to Dr. Gamaliel Bailey. He was the editor of a Washington antislavery newspaper called the *National Era*. As Harriet explained to Dr. Bailey, "I feel now that the time is come when even a woman or a child who can speak a word for freedom and humanity is bound to speak." Dr. Bailey agreed to pay Harriet $300 for the three or four installments she planned to write.

The *National Era* published the first episode of "Uncle Tom's Cabin" on June 5, 1851. By the time Harriet finished the fourth part, the story seemed to have taken on a life of its own. It had to be longer.

Many of the story's characters and incidents were based on Harriet's own memories and experiences. She based her story on slaves and slave owners she had met, stories she had heard, and events she had seen. Tales of a slave fleeing across a frozen river, a visit to a station of the Underground Railroad, the life of Josiah Henson–these all came together in Harriet's story. But she had also researched books, newspapers, and magazines. She had read autobiographies by former slaves, including one by the famous abolitionist Frederick Douglass.

"Uncle Tom's Cabin" was an incredible success. Each issue of the *National Era* that carried

Born a slave in Maryland, Frederick Douglass escaped to the North at the age of 21. In 1841 he gave his first speech at an antislavery meeting in Massachusetts. Afterward, despite threats on his life, he lectured widely about the evils of slavery. An exceptional speaker, writer, and editor, Douglass shared his own slavery experiences in his autobiography.

part of the story sold out. Devoted readers passed on their worn copies to friends and family members. Fan letters poured into the newspaper office as the entire nation followed the riveting story.

Harriet's story follows the lives of several slaves. The book opens on a Kentucky plantation. Mr. Shelby, the plantation owner, is a kind man. But it is Uncle Tom, one of Shelby's slaves, who is the real hero of the book. Tom is a courageous man whose tremendous strength comes from his strong Christian faith. He lives with his wife and children on the plantation. Eliza Harris, also a slave, lives there too. Eliza's husband, George, is owned by a cruel neighbor.

George decides to escape to Canada, and he

tells Eliza he will come back to buy freedom for her and their son, Harry. Soon after George leaves, Eliza learns that Mr. Shelby plans to sell Harry and Uncle Tom to pay his debts.

Eliza warns Tom of the danger and then escapes. Clutching her child in her arms, she heads north. Meanwhile, Tom realizes that he can save the other slaves from being sold if he does not run away. He remains and is sold to the slave trader.

During the steamboat ride taking him further into the South, Tom saves the life of Eva, the daughter of a wealthy man named Augustine St. Clare. In gratitude, St. Clare buys Tom and brings him to his Louisiana plantation.

Meanwhile, slave catchers hunt down Eliza. In one dramatic moment, the desperate young woman escapes, shoeless and bleeding, by crossing the half-frozen Ohio River. Jumping from ice **floe** to ice floe, she struggles toward the safety of the free state on the other side. Eliza and George are reunited. They eventually reach Canada, where they begin a new life together.

Back in the South, Tom has returned to the auction block after the deaths of Eva and her father. The old slave is bought by the cold-hearted Simon Legree.

Eventually Tom defies his cruel owner. He refuses to tell where two other escaped slaves are hiding. A furious Legree orders that Tom be beaten to death. Just before the old slave dies, the son of his first owner, George Shelby, arrives. But he is too late to buy Tom. The young man vows to do everything he can to "drive out this curse of slavery."

A Boston publisher, John P. Jewett, published *Uncle Tom's Cabin: or, Life Among the Lowly* as a book. The first printing of 5,000 copies was released for sale on March 20, 1852. (The publisher chose this date even though the newspaper publication was not scheduled to finish until April 1.)

Within two days, all 5,000 books had sold. To meet the incredible demand, the publisher began running three printing presses 24 hours a

This poster advertises *Uncle Tom's Cabin*. Harriet's novel was one of the best-selling books of the century.

day. In just one year, 300,000 copies of Harriet's book were sold.

This photograph shows Harriet at approximately 41 years old. Because of her book, she became famous all over the world and even met President Abraham Lincoln.

The Woman
Who Made
a War

In *Uncle Tom's Cabin,* the Shelbys, who are slave-owning Southerners, are good people. But because Mr. Shelby needs money, he sells his slaves and destroys their families.

Harriet believed that one of the greatest evils of slavery was the separation of families. She told friends that much of what she put into *Uncle Tom's Cabin* came from the bitter sorrow she felt when her son died. One third of all slave families suffered this kind of loss. Mothers, fathers, and children would often be purchased by separate buyers.

Uncle Tom's Cabin made people in the North

angry. After reading the book, many who had never been to the South or thought much about slavery began to oppose it. The book became so popular in the North that it inspired plays, songs, souvenirs, and even toys.

The book made people in the South angry, too. Southerners were furious that Harriet attacked their way of life. She had never lived in a slave state, they complained. How could she know enough about the slavery system to judge it?

Many slave states passed laws that outlawed buying or selling her book. A free black man in Maryland named Samuel Green was actually sentenced to 10 years in jail for having a copy of *Uncle Tom's Cabin.*

But Harriet knew her story told the truth about

Many popular plays were based on Harriet's novel *Uncle Tom's Cabin*. But producers of these "Tom Shows," as the performances were called, changed the real story. In these shows, instead of having great dignity and faith, the character of Uncle Tom is a foolish old man, over-eager to please others. Because of the Tom Shows, calling a black person an "Uncle Tom" today is considered an insult.

slavery. She put together a book of the facts she had used. *A Key to Uncle Tom's Cabin; Presenting the Original Facts and Documents Upon Which It Is Based* was published in May 1853. The book contained unpublished information and testimonies that supported her statements about how slaves lived—and died. It sold well, although Harriet was disappointed that few people in the South bought it.

Uncle Tom's Cabin made Harriet a celebrity. She was praised around the world, especially in England and France. The book was translated into at least 23 languages, including French, German, Italian, and Portuguese.

Harriet became friends with U.S. Senator Charles Sumner of Massachusetts. He was a strong antislavery leader in Congress. In his speeches, Sumner would often quote from *Uncle Tom's Cabin*.

When Harriet traveled abroad with her husband in 1853 to speak at antislavery societies in Scotland and England, she wrote to Senator Sumner, "The public opinion of the world is our last hope." The people of the British Isles did not disappoint her.

Enthusiastic audiences filled the halls. There were receptions, dinners, and meetings. At one event, Harriet befriended the duchess of Sutherland, who had been an early supporter of the antislavery movement. The duchess gave Harriet a gold bracelet shaped like a slave chain. One of the ten links showed the date when the English abolished slavery in the West Indies. There was a blank space on another link to be inscribed with the date when America's slaves were freed.

The British people presented Harriet with $20,000 to support the antislavery effort. She also received a **petition** calling for the end of slavery. More than half a million British women had signed it.

After returning to the United States, Harriet and Calvin settled into their new home in Andover, Massachusetts. Calvin had accepted a job at Andover Theological Seminary.

Harriet was determined to keep helping the antislavery movement. She wrote pamphlets that were printed and distributed at her expense.

Harriet probably saw this view of the river Thames when she went to London in 1853. Her speaking tour there was very successful.

She sponsored petitions against slavery and sent them to Senator Sumner. She also wrote many articles for abolitionist publications.

The Stowe home in Andover became a hub of antislavery activity. Visitors included William Lloyd Garrison, Frederick Douglass, and many other famous abolitionists. A growing number of people in the North wanted to resist the Fugitive Slave Law.

Proslavery and abolitionist tempers grew hotter. Abolitionists in Kansas wanted the new state to join the Union as a free state. They battled slavery supporters. In May 1856, one fighting abolitionist named John Brown and his followers brutally killed five proslavery men. Brown escaped Kansas, but he would soon be heard from again.

That same month, Senator Charles Sumner made a speech against slavery. In it, he made fun of Senator Pierce Butler of South Carolina. Butler had a speech problem as the result of a stroke.

Congressman Preston Brooks of South Carolina was Butler's nephew. He was so angry about the insult to his uncle that a few days later he beat Sumner with a cane on the Senate floor. Sumner's injuries were so severe that he couldn't return to the Senate for years.

SOUTHERN CHIVALRY _ ARGUMENT versus CLUB'S.

This cartoon shows Congressman Brooks attacking Senator Sumner. This was only one example of tempers flaring up over the issue of slavery.

Harriet had been in the middle of writing a second antislavery novel when Sumner was attacked. Her feelings about the violent assault found their way into the story.

Dred: A Tale of the Great Dismal Swamp was published in 1856. It tells of an escaped slave named Dred who is hiding out with other escaped slaves in the Dismal Swamp of North Carolina. When he tries to start a slave revolt, Dred is shot and killed by white slave hunters.

Dred was not as popular as *Uncle Tom's Cabin*, although 100,000 copies of the book sold during its first four weeks in print.

In the summer of 1857, Harriet's son Henry died in a swimming accident. The news sent her into a depression, but she found comfort in her writing. Her next novel, *The Minister's Wooing*, was not about slavery, but about religious faith.

Harriet was again visiting England with her husband when she heard of more violence in the fight against slavery. Once again,

---

President Lincoln was born in the territory that eventually became the slave state of Kentucky. His wife was a Southerner. But Lincoln did not support slavery. In 1858 he predicted that the nation could not continue if the states had different laws on slavery.

"A house divided against itself cannot stand," he said. "I believe this government cannot endure permanently, half slave and half free. I do not expect the Union to be dissolved—I do not expect the house to fall—but I do expect it will cease to be divided. It will become all one thing, or all the other."

the abolitionist leader involved was John Brown. On October 16, 1859, Brown led 21 men in raiding a federal **arsenal** located at Harpers Ferry, Virginia. With the captured weapons, he planned to start a slave rebellion.

Several people were killed in the fighting. Brown was wounded and captured. Within two months he was hanged. To the abolitionists, John Brown was a hero. Harriet described him as a "brave, good man who calmly gave his life up to a noble effort for human freedom."

The Stowes returned from their trip to England just before the 1860 presidential elections. On November 6, Republican Abraham Lincoln won the race for president. However, before Lincoln had even taken office, seven Southern states seceded from the Union. They did not want anything to do with a nation whose president did not support slavery. South Carolina was the first state to break away. It was quickly followed by Mississippi, Alabama, Georgia, Florida, Louisiana, and Texas.

Nine years after the publication of *Uncle Tom's*

Cabin, the rebellious Southern states formed their own Confederate States of America. The new government elected a president, Jefferson Davis, and a congress. Four more Southern states–Virginia, Arkansas, North Carolina, and Tennessee–soon joined them.

On Friday, April 12, 1861, the South fired on Fort Sumter. This U.S. government fort was located on an island in the Charleston Harbor in South Carolina. Confederate troops soon took over the fort. The Civil War had officially begun.

By that time, two million copies of Harriet's antislavery novel had been bought in the United States. In the decade before the war, millions had read the tale. Many of those readers were the young men who were now volunteering to fight. They were ready to help wipe out slavery.

Harriet and her brother Henry Ward Beecher, now a famous abolitionist preacher, found themselves among the first to support the war. "This is a cause to die for," Harriet wrote in the *National Era*, "and–thanks be to God!–our young men embrace it . . . and are ready to die." Henry preached, "I hold that it is ten times better to have war than to have slavery." Henry's 20-year-old son became one of the first Beechers to enlist. Still, Harriet was surprised when her 21-year-old son, Fred, announced that he planned to join the army.

Fred had been studying at Harvard Medical School, and Harriet wanted him to continue his studies. She was also concerned because he had a problem with alcoholism. But Fred was determined. He signed up for Company A of the First Massachusetts Volunteer Infantry.

Harriet had expected Britain to quickly support the Union. After all, millions of its people had signed the 1853 petition against slavery. But to Harriet's surprise, Queen Victoria announced the country would remain neutral and would even recognize the Confederate States of America.

Most people from both the Northern and the Southern sides believed the Civil War would last only a few months. Harriet also thought the war would end quickly. She believed the Union army would easily overcome the Southern forces.

But in the first major battle of the war, the First Battle of Bull Run, Confederate troops overran the Union forces on a battlefield outside Manassas, Virginia. It was a complete disaster for the Union. The Confederate army went on to defeat the North in many more early battles of the war.

As time went by, both Harriet and her brother Henry became concerned, worrying that the North was not freeing slaves or even talking about it. President Lincoln insisted that the goal of the war was to preserve the Union. He made no mention of ending slavery. In many articles to antislavery newspapers, Harriet criticized the president for not taking a stand against slavery.

Lincoln wanted to keep the rest of the states in the Union, which still contained four slave states—Delaware, Kentucky, Maryland, and Missouri. They were important states on the border between the North and the South. While Lincoln believed that slavery was wrong, he planned to make a statement about ending slavery only when he believed the time was right. The North had to appear forceful before he could make a strong proclamation about slavery.

An important victory for the North came on September 17, 1862. The Battle of Antietam, which was fought near Sharpsburg, Maryland, is remembered as the bloodiest day of the Civil War. Thousands died before the sun set. In the end, the Northern army won.

A few days later, President Lincoln announced he would sign the **Emancipation Proclamation.** This document stated that all slaves in the rebellious states were free as of January 1, 1863. Finally, the meaning of the Civil War had changed. The Union was fighting to end slavery.

Harriet still worried that the president might not really sign the proclamation. She decided to go to Washington to talk to him in person. At the White House, she was introduced to the weary president. With a smile, the six-foot, four-inch president looked down at five-foot-tall Harriet. "So you're the little woman who wrote the book that made this great war," he said. Perhaps he was joking, but there was much truth in his statement.

The president assured Harriet that he would indeed sign the proclamation. He was true to his word. On January 1, 1863, Harriet attended a celebration at the Boston Music Hall. The crowd anxiously awaited the official news of President Lincoln's signing of the Emancipation Proclamation. When the telegraphed announcement came, everyone shouted, stamped, and cheered.

Then someone spotted Harriet in the audience. The crowd began to chant: "Mrs. Stowe! Mrs. Stowe!" Harriet glowed in their warmth and recognition of her part in making the day possible.

The Civil War lasted four long years. By the end of the war, hardly any American family was not mourning the death of a friend or family member. Harriet's son Fred, who was with the Northern army, had received two commendations for bravery in action. He had also commanded a cavalry troop. On July 11, 1863, one week after the Battle of Gettysburg, Harriet learned that her

When President Abraham Lincoln met Harriet, he assured her that he would sign the Emancipation Proclamation.

son had been wounded. A fragment of shell had entered Fred's right ear. By November, the wound still had not healed and he was discharged.

Once again Harriet focused on her family.

Fred had returned home. Calvin was retiring from teaching. And she had a newly built "dream house" in Hartford, Connecticut.

Unfortunately the house was so poorly constructed that Harriet had to start writing to earn money to pay the bills for fixing leaky plumbing, crumbling plaster, and a flooded basement. The talented author produced hundreds of articles and stories. There was nothing she couldn't write about—people, flowers, religion, even pets.

The war raged on until April 9, 1865, when Confederate general Robert E. Lee surrendered to Union general Ulysses S. Grant at the Appomattox Court House in Virginia. The war was officially over. More than 620,000 Americans had died. Brothers had fought brothers, and fathers had fought sons. Cities, farms, and homes had been destroyed. The South was in ruins, and the North was in great debt.

Still, the end of the war was cause for celebration. On April 14, the Stars and Stripes were again raised over Fort Sumter, South Carolina. At the same fort where the great war had begun four years earlier, the bullet-torn flag once lowered in defeat was raised in victory. During the ceremonies, Harriet's brother Henry praised President Lincoln for bringing the nation through the storm of war.

But the violence had not ended. That same April evening, President Lincoln was watching a play at Ford's Theater in Washington, D.C. Suddenly, a man named John Wilkes Booth darted into the theater box and shot the president. Lincoln died the next day. A nation plunged into mourning.

Lincoln's antislavery efforts did not die with him. Congress would eventually pass three **amendments**, or changes, to the U.S. Constitution. These amendments would legally guarantee certain rights for African Americans.

The Thirteenth Amendment (1865) abolished slavery in the United States of America. The Fourteenth Amendment (1868) guaranteed equal protection of the law to all Americans. And the Fifteenth Amendment (1870) gave all male citizens, regardless of race, the right to vote.

Harriet continued to be an active writer as she grew older. She wrote books and magazine articles, but she was always most famous for *Uncle Tom's Cabin*.

The Life of a Writer

With the publication of *Uncle Tom's Cabin*, Harriet had become one of America's best-paid and most famous writers. She continued to write for years to come. From 1862 to 1884, Harriet published nearly a book a year. She also wrote articles for the newly started *Atlantic Monthly* magazine and for papers edited by her brother Henry—the *Independent* and the *Christian Union*.

After the war, Harriet wrote six more novels. One, *Oldtown Folks*, was based on stories her father had told. The other, *Poganuc People*, was based on her own life and New England people she knew.

Once the war was over, Harriet tried to help Fred. Even though he had recovered from his head injury, he had other troubles. The worst was his alcoholism. In an effort to give Fred a steady job, Harriet bought a 200-acre orange grove in Florida for him to manage. On her first visit there, Harriet delighted in the mild southern climate. She and Calvin purchased a home near the town of Mandarin. For the next several years, they spent the winter in Florida and returned to Hartford each spring.

Fred did a good job running the Florida plantation for about a year. Then he fell back into bad habits. In 1871 he sailed to San Francisco, California, and disappeared. Harriet and Calvin tried to find what had happened to their son, but they never heard from him again.

At 61, Harriet took up public speaking. It was now finally acceptable for a woman to speak in public. Although at first Harriet was shy before an audience, in time she grew more comfortable. She was, after all, the daughter of a preacher. Her

Harriet retired to a New England town like this one. She lived a long, interesting life and died peacefully at age 85.

readings from *Uncle Tom's Cabin* drew many people.

In 1884 the Stowes gave up winters in Florida and took up permanent residence in Hartford. Two years later, Calvin died after a long illness.

Toward the end of Harriet's life, her youngest son, Charles Edward, helped her organize her letters and journals. The resulting biography, *The Life of Harriet Beecher Stowe,* was published in 1889. Soon afterward, Harriet suffered a mild stroke.

On July 1, 1896, at 85, Harriet died. Her will said that the gold slave bracelet given to her by the duchess of Sutherland would go to one of her daughters. The blank link had been engraved with the date of the Emancipation Proclamation.

Harriet's greatest triumph had been to help end slavery. In doing so she also became one of the best-known American writers of the 1800s. This "little woman" wrote at a time when few women were writers and the voices of few women were heard.

Harriet produced what has been called the best example of antislavery literature. With her words, she changed how the world thought. By writing *Uncle Tom's Cabin,* Harriet Beecher Stowe changed American history.

GLOSSARY

abolitionists–people who worked to end slavery in the United States

accursed–being under evil or misfortune

amendment–legal change or correction

arsenal–a place for storing or making arms and ammunition

autobiography–the story of a person's life as told by that person

bankruptcy–the state of being legally declared unable to pay debts

cholera–a deadly sickness that involves vomiting, diarrhea, and chills

Congregationalist–a type of Protestant church

emancipated–set free

Emancipation Proclamation–a document signed in 1863 that freed all slaves in the Confederate States

floe–floating chunk of ice

free state–a state that did not allow slavery

fugitive–a runaway, or a person who has escaped

Fugitive Slave Act–a law passed in 1850 that kept Northerners from helping escaped slaves

legislators–people who make or pass laws

libeling–making untrue statements about someone that are damaging to that person's character

parsonage–the house provided by a church for its minister

petition–a signed, written request asking for an action to be taken

plantation–a large estate or farm on which crops are grown and harvested by workers who live there

radical–favoring basic social or economic structure changes

secede–to break away from

sketch–a short piece of writing

slaughterhouse–a place where animals are killed for food

slave state–a state in which slavery was legal

suffrage–gaining the right to vote

tuberculosis–a disease of the lungs

Underground Railroad–a network of places and people helping slaves escape to freedom

CHRONOLOGY

1811	Born on June 14 in Litchfield, Connecticut, to Lyman and Roxana Foote Beecher.
1816	Mother dies of tuberculosis.
1832	Family moves to Cincinnati, Ohio.
1836	Marries Calvin Stowe.
1843	Publishes collection of short stories, *The Mayflower: Sketches of Scenes and Characters Among the Descendants of the Pilgrims.*
1850	Fugitive Slave Act is passed; moves to Brunswick, Maine.
1852	*Uncle Tom's Cabin* is published, after first appearing in small sections every week in a newspaper.
1853	*A Key to Uncle Tom's Cabin* is published; moves to Andover, Massachusetts.
1856	Publishes second antislavery novel, *Dred: A Tale of the Great Dismal Swamp.*
1861	The Civil War begins.
1862	Meets with President Abraham Lincoln to request that he sign the Emancipation Proclamation.
1863	President Lincoln signs the Emancipation Proclamation; Harriet moves to Hartford, Connecticut.

1865 The Civil War ends; President Lincoln is assassinated; Congress passes Thirteenth Amendment to the Constitution, which outlaws slavery.

1878 Last novel, *Poganuc People,* is published.

1886 Husband dies.

1896 Dies in Hartford, Connecticut.

CIVIL WAR TIME LINE

1860   Abraham Lincoln is elected president of the United States on November 6. During the next few months, Southern states begin to break away from the Union.

1861   On April 12, the Confederates attack Fort Sumter, South Carolina, and the Civil War begins. Union forces are defeated in Virginia at the First Battle of Bull Run (First Manassas) on July 21 and withdraw to Washington, D.C.

1862   Robert E. Lee is placed in command of the main Confederate army in Virginia in June. Lee defeats the Army of the Potomac at the Second Battle of Bull Run (Second Manassas) in Virginia on August 29–30. On September 17, Union general George B. McClellan turns back Lee's first invasion of the North at Antietam Creek near Sharpsburg, Maryland. It is the bloodiest day of the war.

1863   On January 1, President Lincoln issues the Emancipation Proclamation, freeing slaves in Southern states. Between May 1–6, Lee wins an important victory at Chancellorsville, but key Southern commander Thomas J. "Stonewall" Jackson dies from wounds. In June, Union forces hold the city of Vicksburg, Mississippi, under siege. The people of Vicksburg surrender on July 4. Lee's second invasion of the North during July 1–3 is decisively turned back at Gettysburg, Pennsylvania.

1864   General Grant is made supreme Union commander
        on March 9. Following a series of costly battles, on
        June 19 Grant successfully encircles Lee's troops in
        Petersburg, Virginia. A siege of the town lasts nearly
        a year. Union general William Sherman captures
        Atlanta on September 2 and begins the "March to the
        Sea," a campaign of destruction across Georgia and
        South Carolina. On November 8, Abraham Lincoln
        wins reelection as president.

1865   On April 2, Petersburg, Virginia, falls to the Union.
        Lee attempts to reach Confederate forces in North
        Carolina but is gradually surrounded by Union troops.
        Lee surrenders to Grant on April 9 at Appomattox,
        Virginia, ending the war. Abraham Lincoln is assassinated
        by John Wilkes Booth on April 14.

FURTHER READING

Bland, Celia. *Harriet Beecher Stowe.* Philadelphia: Chelsea House Publishers, 1993.

Chang, Ina. *A Separate Battle: Women and the Civil War.* New York: Puffin Books, 1996.

Coil, Suzanne M. *Harriet Beecher Stowe.* New York: Franklin Watts, 1993.

Fritz, Jean. *Harriet Beecher Stowe and the Beecher Preachers.* New York: G. P. Putnam's Sons, 1994.

Gorrell, Gena K. *North Star to Freedom: The Story of the Underground Railroad.* New York: Delacorte Press, 1997.

Hakim, Joy. *War, Terrible War 1860–1865.* New York: Oxford University Press, 1999.

Johnston, Norma. *Harriet: The Life and World of Harriet Beecher Stowe.* New York: Four Winds Press, 1994.

Rogers, James T. *The Antislavery Movement.* New York: Facts on File, 1994.

Tackach, James. *The Emancipation Proclamation: Abolishing Slavery in the South.* San Diego, Calif.: Lucent Books, 1999.

INDEX

PICTURE CREDITS

ABOUT THE AUTHOR

LEEANNE GELLETLY is an editor and writer who has worked in publishing in New York and Washington, D.C. She now lives in Berwyn, Pennsylvania, with her husband, Dave Clark, and three sons, Jamie, Travis, and Philip.

Senior Consulting Editor **ARTHUR M. SCHLESINGER, JR.** is the leading American historian of our time. He won the Pulitzer Prize for his book *The Age of Jackson* (1945), and again for *A Thousand Days* (1965). This chronicle of the Kennedy Administration also won a National Book Award. He has written many other books, including a multi-volume series, *The Age of Roosevelt.* Professor Schlesinger is the Albert Schweitzer Professor of the Humanities at the City University of New York, and has been involved in several other Chelsea House projects, including the COLONIAL LEADERS series of biographies on the most prominent figures of early American history.